OUR LIVING WORLD

Birds

By **Edward R. Ricciuti**

With Illustrations by William Simpson

Series Editor: Vincent Marteka

Introduction by John Behler, *New York Zoological Society*

A BLACKBIRCH PRESS BOOK

WOODBRIDGE, CONNECTICUT

Published by Blackbirch Press, Inc.
One Bradley Road, Suite 205
Woodbridge, CT 06525

©1993 Blackbirch Press, Inc.
First Edition

Printed in Canada

10 9 8 7 6 5 4 3 2 1

Editorial Director: Bruce Glassman
Editor: Geraldine C. Fox
Editorial Assistant: Michelle Spinelli
Design Director: Sonja Kalter
Production: Sandra Burr, Rudy Raccio

Library of Congress Cataloging-in-Publication Data

Ricciuti, Edward R.
   Birds / by Edward R. Ricciuti.—1st ed.
     p.   cm. — (Our living world)
   Includes bibliographical references and index.
   Summary: Examines the physical structure, metabolism, and life cycle of birds and discusses how they fit into the food chain.
   ISBN 1-56711-038-X   ISBN 1-56711-053-3 (Trade)
   1. Birds—Juvenile literature. [1. Birds.] I. Title. II. Series.
QL676.2.R53   1993
598—dc20   92-44037
                                                  CIP
                                                  AC

Contents

What Does It Mean to Be "Alive"?

Introduction by John Behler,
New York Zoological Society

One summer morning, as I was walking through a beautiful field, I was inspired to think about what it really means to be "alive." Part of the answer, I came to realize, was right in front of my eyes.

The meadow was ablaze with color, packed with wildflowers at the height of their blooming season. A multitude of insects, warmed by the sun's early-morning rays, began to stir. Painted turtles sunned themselves on an old mossy log in a nearby pond. A pair of wood ducks whistled a call as they flew overhead, resting near a shagbark hickory on the other side of the pond.

As I wandered through this unspoiled habitat, I paused at a patch of milkweed to look for monarch-butterfly caterpillars, which depend on the milkweed's leaves for food. Indeed, the caterpillars were there, munching away. Soon these larvae would spin their cocoons, emerge as beautiful orange-and-black butterflies, and begin a fantastic 1,500-mile (2,400-kilometer) migration to wintering grounds in Mexico. It took biologists nearly one hundred years to unravel the life history of these butterflies. Watching them in the milkweed patch made me wonder how much more there is to know about these insects and all the other living organisms in just that one meadow.

The patterns of the natural world have often been likened to a spider's web, and for good reason. All life on Earth is interconnected in an elegant yet surprisingly simple design, and each living thing is an essential part of that design. To understand biology and the functions of living things, biologists have spent a lot of time looking at the differences among organisms. But in order to understand the very nature of living things, we must first understand what they have in common.

The butterfly larvae and the milkweed—and all animals and plants, for that matter—are made up of the same basic elements. These elements are obtained, used, and eliminated by every living thing in a series of chemical activities called metabolism.

Every molecule of every living tissue must contain carbon. During photosynthesis, green plants take in carbon dioxide from the atmosphere. Within their chlorophyll-filled leaves, in the presence of sunlight, the carbon dioxide is combined with water to form sugar—nature's most basic food. Animals need carbon, too. To grow and function, animals must eat plants or other animals that have fed on plants in order to obtain carbon. When plants and animals die, bacteria and fungi help to break down their tissues. This allows the carbon in plants and animals to be recycled. Indeed, the carbon in your body—and everyone else's body—may once have been inside a dinosaur, a giant redwood, or a monarch butterfly!

All life also needs nitrogen. Nitrogen is an essential component of protoplasm, the complex of chemicals that makes up living cells. Animals acquire nitrogen in the same manner as they acquire carbon dioxide: by eating plants or other animals that have eaten plants. Plants, however, must rely on nitrogen-fixing bacteria in the soil to absorb nitrogen from the atmosphere and convert it into proteins. These proteins are then absorbed from the soil by plant roots.

Living things start life as a single cell. The process by which cells grow and reproduce to become a specific organism—whether the organism is an oak tree or a whale—is controlled by two basic substances called deoxyribonucleic acid (DNA) and ribonucleic acid (RNA). These two chemicals are the building blocks of genes that determine how an organism looks, grows, and functions. Each organism has a unique pattern of DNA and RNA in its genes. This pattern determines all the characteristics of a living thing. Each species passes its unique pattern from generation to generation. Over many billions of years, a process involving genetic mutation and natural selection has allowed species to adapt to a constantly changing environment by evolving—changing genetic patterns. The living creatures we know today are the results of these adaptations.

Reproduction and growth are important to every species, since these are the processes by which new members of a species are created. If a species cannot reproduce and adapt, or if it cannot reproduce fast enough to replace those members that die, it will become extinct (no longer exist).

In recent years, biologists have learned a great deal about how living things function. But there is still much to learn about nature. With high-technology equipment and new information, exciting discoveries are being made every day. New insights and theories quickly make many biology textbooks obsolete. One thing, however, will forever remain certain: As living things, we share an amazing number of characteristics with other forms of life. As animals, our survival depends upon the food and functions provided by other animals and plants. As humans—who can understand the similarities and interdependence among living things—we cannot help but feel connected to the natural world, and we cannot forget our responsibility to protect it. It is only through looking at, and understanding, the rest of the natural world that we can truly appreciate what it means to be "alive."

Birds:
The Overview

 Swallows zoom through the air and perch on telephone wires. Robins probe lawns for earthworms. Crows fly overhead. Chickadees and blue jays come to bird feeders.

You probably see birds more than any other wild animals. Birds are everywhere, even in the middle of a big city. There, pigeons thrive, and starlings and house sparrows are also very common.

Some cities, especially those with lots of parks, are full of birds. At one time of year or another, for instance, more than 400 species of birds can be seen in New York City. That is more than half of the approximately 700 species in the United States and Canada.

What Are Birds?

Birds are one of five groups (classes) of vertebrates, or animals with a backbone. The other classes are fishes, amphibians, reptiles, and mammals.

Opposite:
A tidal mud flat is invaded by a flock of wading birds in search of food. Birds are among the most common wild animals in our world.

Amazing Feets

The foot of an animal tells much about where and how it lives. Most birds have four toes. Generally, three toes point forward and one toe points backward. Usually, the forward toes are much longer than the rear toe. But there are always exceptions. The toes of a hawk's foot are of similar length, which helps the bird hold on to prey. The woodpecker's toes also are all about the same length; two point forward, two point backward. This helps the woodpecker brace itself on a tree trunk. An ostrich has only two toes, but each is massive, helping the ostrich run up to 40 miles (64 kilometers) an hour. Ducks have the common bird-toe arrangement, but their front three toes are connected by a web that is specially designed for swimming.

Many things make birds special. They are the only group of vertebrates for which flying is a basic ability. Almost all birds fly. Bats, which are mammals, can fly, too. So can one species of small fish from South America. It vibrates its fins to lift itself above the water for a short distance. But these are the only two non-bird vertebrates that can fly.

The Wonder of Adaptation

Adaptations are physical and behavioral traits that help a species survive. Body shape is an adaptation. So are structures such as wings. Adaptations happen by chance as a species evolves. The adaptations that best help a species to survive are those that are passed to future generations. Species that adapt to their environment continue to exist. Those that do not become extinct (no longer exist).

Adaptations for Flight

Several adaptations enable a bird to fly. Flying takes enormous muscle power. A bird has about 175 different muscles. Those that enable a bird to fly are not in the wings. They are mainly in its chest. These muscles can make up more than a third of a bird's weight.

The breastbone of a bird is the biggest bone in its skeleton. It needs to be big to support all the muscles required for flying. The top of the breastbone has a high ridge, like the ridge on the bottom of a boat. The ridge provides a surface for the attachment of muscles.

Have you ever found a wishbone when eating chicken or turkey? This bone is composed of a bird's two collar bones. They are joined together at their base. The wishbone helps support the bird's wings during flight.

The bones of a bird are not solid. Inside, they are honeycombed with tiny air spaces. These spaces make a bird's skeleton lightweight, which is another important adaptation for flight.

Feathers also help a bird fly. They compress when a bird is moving through the air. That way, the bird's body takes on a more streamlined shape. A streamlined shape gets less air resistance, or "drag." With less drag, it is easier to fly. That is why streamlining decreases the amount of energy a bird needs to fly.

Wings in Flight

The wings of a bird act like the wings and propeller of an airplane. They lift the bird off the ground and provide forward movement. The function of the inner half of a wing corresponds to that of the human arm. The outer part of a wing is like the human hand. During flight, the outer part of the wing moves in a half circle, while the wing tip moves in a figure eight. Both movements lift the bird up and propel it forward. The inner half adds to the lift.

The shape of a wing also helps in flight. The leading edge is thicker than the trailing edge. The leading edge moves air aside; the thinner trailing edge lets air slip by with little resistance. The upper side of the wing is curved. The underside is flat. Air passes over the top of the wing more quickly than along the bottom of the wing. The faster air lowers the air pressure above the wing. The higher pressure under the wing pushes against the

The flight of a bird, such as the mallard, involves a semicircular wing motion with downward and upward strokes. During the downstroke, the primary feathers at the wingtips twist, thrusting the bird forward. During the upstroke, the wing feathers part, making it easier to raise the wing.

Wing Movement

1
2
3
4
5
6

Water Wings: Facts About Penguins

The breastbone of flightless ground birds, such as the ostrich, lacks a high ridge. The penguin is flightless, too, but its breastbone resembles that of flying birds. Penguins use their wings to swim underwater. It is almost like flying beneath the surface of the sea. So they need big chest muscles, like a bird that flies in the air. The webbed feet of a penguin act like the rudders of a boat. They enable the penguin to twist and turn when it chases fish to eat. Quick movement also helps to outmaneuver enemies, such as big sea lions. Think about the shape of a penguin. It resembles that of a sea lion. Both are streamlined for underwater travel. Like penguins, sea lions can twist and turn very easily underwater. They use their flippers to swim and maneuver. The water animals with the most streamlined shapes are fish. They need all the help they can get to escape penguins, seals, and sea lions!

Many people think penguins live only in the frozen Antarctic. While it is true that several species of penguins live there, some also inhabit the coasts of New Zealand, Australia, South Africa, and South America. One penguin species lives on the Galápagos Islands, in the tropical Pacific. That is just south of the equator, at the midpoint of the globe. No penguins, however, live north of the equator.

wing, providing more lift to the bird, and therefore helping it to stay up in the air.

How do a bird's feathers help it to get that lift, defying gravity and preventing it from falling to the ground? Large feathers called primaries cover the outer half of the wing. On the downflap, the primaries flatten and overlap. This creates a large, unbroken surface that supports the bird against the air. It helps lift the bird. Meanwhile, the tips of the primaries twist. Each tip acts like a propeller, moving the bird up and ahead.

On the upstroke, the primaries part. Air slips through them, making it easier to raise the wing. The wing tip presses up and back against the air, pushing the bird ahead.

Feathers Are Special

If anything makes a bird special, the feathers do. Only birds have feathers. Feathers are flexible and are extraordinarily light. But they also are durable. No other natural material of an equal size and weight is as strong as a feather.

Birds are covered with an amazing number of feathers. A little songbird can have more than 4,000 of them. A swan can have more than 25,000 feathers! Some feathers are huge and flowing—like the plumes of an ostrich. Others are hair-like—like those of the big cassowary and the small kiwi.

Feathers may appear to cover the bird's entire body, but they don't. They grow only on special areas of skin, which are separated by bare areas. The central part of the feather is its shaft. It is fringed on each side by barbs, the "feathery" part of the feather.

Healthy feathers are almost totally waterproof. They are also great insulators against cold. Do you know what's inside your down winter jacket? It's probably goose down. (The soft, simple feathers of a bird are called down.) Air trapped in feathers helps keep out cold. In chilly weather, birds puff out their feathers to trap more air.

Birds are covered with an amazing number of feathers. A bird such as the flamingo can have more than 25,000 feathers on its body.

Hover Lover

The wing of a hummingbird is different from that of most other birds. It is rigid, and it swivels at the shoulder. This enables the hummingbird to hover like a helicopter. It can even fly backward. A hummingbird's wings beat an average of 30 to 50 times a second.

Birds of Different Feathers

The ostrich is the largest living bird. It weighs an average of 300 pounds (136 kilograms). It stands about 8 feet (2.5 meters) high, and its egg is bigger than a softball! The Helena's hummingbird of Cuba is the smallest living bird. It weighs an average of .07 ounce (2 grams). That's less than a Ping-Pong ball weighs. There is a certain point at which a bird's body is too heavy for it to fly. The largest flying birds weigh somewhat less than about 40 pounds (18 kilograms). The largest may be the great bustard of Eurasia. Some have weighed in at more than 37 pounds (17 kilograms). Birds that fly and soar for great distances can have immense wings. A wandering albatross, a seabird, has been measured with a wing span of almost 13 feet (4 meters).

Ostrich

The Evolution of Birds

Scientists believe feathers developed from the scales that cover reptiles. Why? Because birds evolved, or developed, from reptiles. That happened more than 130 million years ago.

Fossils indicate that birds descend from a group of reptiles called archosaurs. This is a Greek term that means "ruling reptiles." The group got its name because it included the dinosaurs. Some scientists playfully call birds "feathered dinosaurs." In fact, the first known bird, archaeopteryx, had a skeleton that was similar to that of a small dinosaur.

Birds, however, most likely did not evolve from the ancient flying reptiles, the pterosaurs. The ancestors of birds were small reptiles that walked on their rear legs. More than 200 million years ago, some of these reptiles began to climb trees. Eventually, they began to glide among the branches. Over millions of years, the process of adaptation enabled them to fly.

The Wide Variety of Birds

About 8,600 species of birds exist today. Scientists commonly divide them into 28 different groups, called orders. Species in an order are more closely related to each other than to those in other orders.

Ducks, geese, swans, and a tropical bird called the screamer make up an order. Pheasants and turkeys make up another order. The ostrich is an order all to itself.

The largest order is the "perching birds," also known as songbirds. Most birds, in fact, belong to this order—about 6,000 species in all.

Perching birds get their name because of the way their toes lock onto a branch. Tendons run down the leg of a perching bird all the way to its toe tips. When a bird flies or walks, its tendons are relaxed. When a bird perches, it bends its legs. The tendons then tighten and pull in the toes to lock onto a branch.

Perching birds are not the only ones that have toes that can lock, but this ability is most highly developed in them. Hawks and eagles, for example, have a similar ability for locking onto prey.

The largest order of birds is the perching birds, named for the way in which their toes lock onto branches and other long, thin structures.

Where Birds Live

Birds live almost everywhere on the Earth. They are found on all continents. Even the most remote islands have birds. Some birds spend almost all their lives at sea. Other birds live in wetlands, deserts, jungles, plains, suburbs, and cities. Thousands of bird species inhabit forests. Tropical forests have the greatest variety of birds. About 2,500 species live year-round in the forests of tropical America.

Because they can fly, some species of birds travel great distances during their lifetimes. Many species migrate (seasonally relocate) each year, flying thousands of miles to find warmer climates.

Eight Orders of Living Birds

Scientists have classified the approximately 8,600 species of birds into different orders. An order is a grouping of organisms that share more traits with one another than with other organisms. The specific classifications vary among scientists, depending upon how each order is defined.

Common Traits of **FALCONIFORMES**
• Birds of prey.
• Worldwide in most habitats.
• Excellent fliers.
• Feed mostly on small mammals, reptiles, fish, carrion, and other birds.
Example: **OSPREY**

Common Traits of **PASSERIFORMES**
• Perching birds.
• All are land birds.
• Most are small in size.
Example: **BLUE JAY**

Common Traits of **PICIFORMES**
• Forest and marshland birds.
• Many nest in tree cavities.
Example: **TOUCAN**

Common Traits of **APTERYGIFORMES**
• Flightless birds.
• Lack the bony breastbone ridge to support wings.
• Related to Struthioniformes.
Example: **KIWI**

Common Traits of **STRIGIFORMES**
• Nocturnal (most active during nighttime).
• Mostly forest dwellers.
• Excellent hearing and eyesight adapted for nighttime hunting.
Example: **OWL**

Common Traits of **STRUTHIONIFORMES**
• Large in size.
• Flightless.
• Swift runners.
• Lack the bony breastbone ridge
  to support wings.
Example: **OSTRICH**

Common Traits of **APODIFORMES**
• Small in size.
• Highly specialized fliers.
• Many inhabit tropical regions.
Example: **HUMMINGBIRD**

Common Traits of **ANSERIFORMES**
• Waterfowl.
• Most are excellent fliers.
Example: **WOOD DUCK**

15

The Senses:
How Birds React

Soaring almost a mile high, a turkey vulture sees a dead rabbit in a forest below. The dead rabbit is food. The vulture zeroes in and heads for the ground.

At another location, in the pitch-black night, a barn owl sits on its perch, waiting. Below, a white-footed mouse scurries for a hiding place. It makes no more noise than a dry leaf blown by a breeze across a lawn. In the blackness, a human would not see it. But the owl swoops down from its perch and catches the mouse effortlessly in its curved claws.

Birds can accomplish such feats because of their sense organs. Like all living things, birds rely on their senses to gather information about their environment. Sense organs detect changes in surroundings. A change that is picked up by the sense organs is sent like a message to the brain. This message is called a stimulus.

Opposite:
Owls have large eyes that provide them with extraordinary vision. Like all living things, birds rely on their senses to react to their surroundings.

Sense organs receive stimuli non-stop. Stimuli can be gradual, like the cycle of day and night, or they can be quick, like a mouse running for cover.

Whether fast or slow, stimuli are channeled through an organism's nervous system. Sense organs are the nervous system's receivers. They send the information they receive through nerve channels to the brain. The brain processes the information and sends out orders to the body. If all is working properly, the body reacts to the brain's orders with an action that is appropriate to the situation.

Here's an example of how a human reacts to a stimulus. You are at bat in a baseball game. The pitcher throws the ball, but it goes off course, toward your head. In a flash, you see the ball coming at you. That information zooms to your brain. Your brain immediately tells your body to jump aside. Once you're out of danger, your brain tells your body it is okay to relax.

Now imagine you are a robin hopping across a lawn. A cat creeps up 10 yards in front of you. You freeze. If the cat comes closer, you are in the air in an instant. Your reaction to the stimulus received by your sense organs saves your life.

Sense organs are a key to survival. They help an animal find food, locate a mate, find its way around, and escape danger.

Like all animals, birds rely on five major senses: sight, smell, touch, taste, and hearing. The most important sense to a bird is sight.

How Birds See

Vision relays information to the brain very quickly. It is understandable that vision is the sense used most by creatures that move rapidly through the air. The section of the vertebrate brain that is involved in vision is called the optic lobe. For their size, birds have the biggest optic lobes of all vertebrates.

The eyes of a bird are also very large. Some birds have eyes more than 12 times bigger than those of humans, relative to overall body size. Of all the land animals, including humans, eagles, owls, and ostriches have the biggest eyes relative to their size.

Big eyes contain more vision cells than small eyes. And more vision cells means better vision. A hunting bird can have more than a million vision cells in one eye. The human eye averages only about 200,000.

How the Eye Works

All vertebrate eyes work the same way, basically like a camera. The center of the front of the eye is covered by the lens. The lens is clear and permits light to pass through. Light rays enter the eye through the lens. The light then registers an image on the retina, which is a coating at the back of the eyeball. The retina is covered with vision cells called rods and cones (their names come from their shapes). The retina works like a camera's film, which registers an image when it is exposed to light. Messages from the rods and cones are sent along the optic nerve to the brain. There, the image on the retina is developed into a picture. The lens of a bird's eye is flexible. It bulges to better focus on nearby objects, and it flattens for distance. Human lenses (and those of all vertebrates) work in a similar way.

Most people think that birds can see much better than humans. That's true for many big birds, such as hawks,

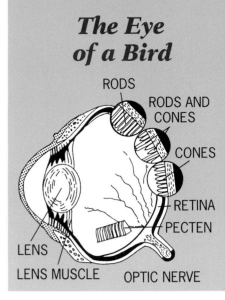

The Eye of a Bird

RODS
RODS AND CONES
CONES
RETINA
PECTEN
LENS
LENS MUSCLE
OPTIC NERVE

The eye of a bird—like that of a human or other vertebrate—works something like a camera. Light enters through a lens in the front of the eye and registers an image on a light-sensitive coating on the retina at the back of the eye. Vision cells called rods and cones help the bird to see in varying degrees of light and aid in distinguishing detail and color.

Quality of vision is related to eye size and to the relative size of the eyes to the body. Of all the land animals, including humans, eagles, owls, and ostriches have the biggest eyes relative to their size.

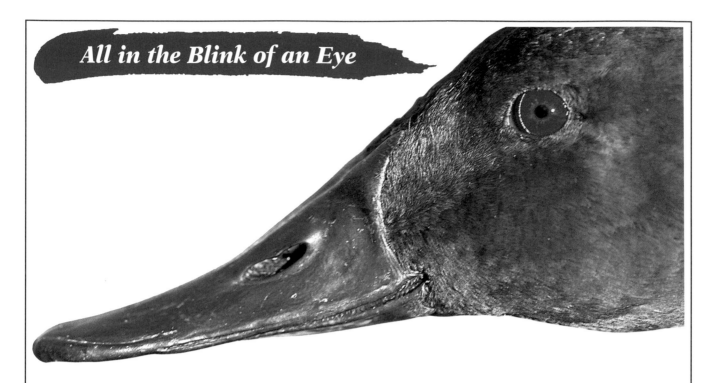

All in the Blink of an Eye

In the last minute, you have blinked about 22 times. Blinking helps keep eyes moist and clean. When you blink, your vision is out of commission for just a fraction of a second. But a bird can blink without ever losing sight. A bird's eye has a third eyelid called the nictitating membrane. This membrane is transparent. It moves from side to side across the eye. Because it is clear, a bird can blink without closing its eyes. For birds that dive underwater, the membrane acts like a diver's face mask, protecting the eye and eliminating the distortion of water. Many reptiles also have a nictitating membrane in their eyes.

eagles, and falcons, but not for many small birds. Visual ability is a matter of eye size. A hawk's eye, for example, is much bigger than a chickadee's.

What a bird's eye does best is to instantly pick up sharp images while scanning a large area. In comparison, a human eye would have to scan the same area slowly, a bit at a time, to see things as clearly.

Hawks and eagles also seem to see sharply over greater distances than other vertebrates. Some scientists think this may be due to a structure called the pecten, which supplies extra blood to the eye.

Field of Vision

The area over which an animal can see without moving its head is called its field of vision. Fields of vision vary among birds. So does the area of the field of vision in which the eye can judge distance and depth (called binocular vision). All of these skills depend on the placement of the eyes in the head. The owl has eyes in the front of its head. This limits its field of vision to what is in front. But it gives the owl a large area of binocular vision, an important feature for a hunting bird. Prey are usually in front of an owl, and the ability to judge depth and distance keeps the owl on target while hunting and capturing.

The woodcock pulls worms out of the ground with its long bill. When feeding, its head is down. For many animals, this is a difficult position from which to see enemies. But the woodcock's eyes are on the side of its head. Its field of vision is a full circle. It can even see enemies that are behind it. The woodcock has little binocular vision, but it doesn't need much. Its food is usually right under its bill!

Birds have a full range of color vision. The cones are the vision cells that are sensitive to color (the rods are for black and white only). The cones are more numerous than the rods in a bird's eye. The color of a bird's body plays an important role in its life. Birds use colors to recognize other members of their species and to find a mate.

The woodcock has eyes on the side of its head so it can see enemies behind it as it feeds on worms and other insects from the ground.

How Birds Hear

You cannot see them, but birds have ears that are much like human ears. What birds do not have is a large outer ear. A large outer ear would create air friction and would require more energy in flight. A bird's ears are under feathers on the side of its head. The inside of a bird's ear is much like yours, but simpler. Mostly, however, it works the same way.

Sound is produced by vibrating objects and travels in the form of waves. An eardrum picks up the vibrations of sound waves. A bone that is located

The Senses: How Birds React

I'm Owl Ears

An owl's eyes are very sensitive to light. Owls can see at night, but they cannot see in total darkness. In complete darkness, the owl's ears take over. The two ears of an owl are not exactly opposite one another like yours. Instead, they are offset, and one is higher on the head than the other. A particular sound wave reaches one ear before it reaches the other. Which ear hears first depends on the direction of the sound. This helps an owl pinpoint the source of a sound. Barn owls can catch mice by sound alone.

behind the eardrum carries the vibrations. Next, the vibrations are transmitted to a tube-like structure called the cochlea. Messages from the cochlea are sent along a nerve to the brain, which interprets the signals as sound.

Most birds cannot hear as wide a range of sounds as humans can, but their hearing is very sensitive. They can hear bits of bird song that escape human ears. This ability is important because song is a very useful form of communication for birds.

Let's Talk Birds

Parrot

The family of birds with the most highly developed brains are crows, jays, and their relatives. Parrots also have highly developed brains. All of these birds are known for their ability to mimic a variety of complex sounds including human speech.

Many birds can mimic other birds. The mockingbird gets its name because of its ability to "mock," or imitate, other bird species. Bluejays can imitate the call of the red-tailed hawk. They do it as an alarm call whenever a hawk comes near.

The parrot has a fleshy tongue that is very sensitive. A parrot's tongue helps it to pick up small pieces of food and probably plays a part in helping the bird imitate human speech.

Parrots can be trained to use many words, sometimes a hundred or even more. Some trainers claim that parrots can be taught to count and to recognize colors and shapes with speech commands. Parrots often begin to talk once they become attached to a person. They sense that talking will attract their owner's attention and will provide a way in which to interact.

Although most birds rely very little on their sense of smell, the kiwi has developed a keen sense of smell, which enables it to hunt in the dark.

Taste, Smell, and Touch

The majority of birds seem to rely relatively little on their senses of taste, smell, and touch.

A bird tastes with taste buds that are similar to a human's. The buds are located in the bird's mouth, but birds have far fewer taste buds than mammals.

A bird's organs of smell are chambers above the roof of its mouth. These organs open into the mouth and nostrils. The nostrils are on the bill.

Although most birds do not rely heavily on smell, nature is full of exceptions. The kiwi, a flightless bird from New Zealand, hunts worms by smell. Its nostrils are at the top of its beak, which is long, like a woodcock's. The kiwi has small eyes and therefore poor vision. But kiwis hunt in the dark of night. Because of the kiwi's specific pattern of hunting and living, it relies more on its ability to smell and less on its eyes for vision.

Birds sense touch much like humans do. Nerve endings in a bird's skin relay stimuli to its brain. The feathers on a bird can mask its sense of touch. That is why a bird's nerve endings tend to be more densely concentrated in those areas of the body that are lightly feathered or bare.

3

Metabolism: How Birds Function

Birds need lots of energy to fly. Like mammals, birds can maintain their body temperature regardless of surrounding conditions. The body temperature of birds is higher than that of mammals. The normal temperature of birds can be as high as 111 degrees F. (44 degrees C.). Especially in cold weather, it takes a great deal of energy to maintain such a high temperature.

Making energy requires fuel. For a bird, or any other living thing, the fuel is food. Living organisms break down food and convert it to energy, which then enables the body to function and grow.

Getting, storing, and converting food to energy are chemical processes that keep all living things alive. Eliminating wastes that are created from these processes is also essential. Together, these activities are called metabolism. Because they need so much energy, birds have a high rate of metabolism.

The Basics of Metabolism

The basics of animal metabolism are fairly simple. First, an animal eats food. Then the food is digested. That means the food is broken down by certain chemicals into substances the body can use.

Meanwhile, the animal takes in oxygen through its breathing, or respiratory, system. Oxygen combines with digested food to produce energy. Without oxygen, the body cannot "burn" its food as fuel. Oxygen aids in releasing energy for many things. Wood will not burn without oxygen. In the presence of oxygen, however, burning wood releases heat and light energy.

A wood fire also produces ash. Ash is a waste product, left over after all the fuel has been used. An animal's body produces a waste gas when it makes energy. This gas is called carbon dioxide. Digestion also produces solid wastes, or feces. Urine is the liquid waste left over after drinking and digesting.

Metabolism is complex. Many different chemical processes must interact to keep it working smoothly. As long as metabolism works, an organism can do what it needs in order to live. If metabolism breaks down or stops, it means an end to the life of any living thing.

What Birds Eat

If you have ever seen a crowded bird feeder hanging outside, you know many birds eat seeds. But that's only part of what birds eat. All bird species combined eat as many different kinds of food as humans do.

Birds of prey eat meat. The sharp-shinned hawk feeds largely on songbirds. It often ambushes them at bird feeders.

The golden eagle eats mostly mammals, such as rabbits and large rodents. Owls feed on ground birds

and several kinds of small mammals. The great horned owl, the second largest owl in North America, often dines on skunks.

Fish and other aquatic creatures are the main diet for many birds. Herons eat fish, frogs, and salamanders. Penguins live mostly on fish, squid, and small crustaceans that are similar to shrimp. Some penguins rely on the same shrimp-like crustaceans for food as do the great whales. Even though little penguins and huge blue whales compete for the same food, both are able to survive.

Gulls snatch small fish from the water. They also snatch insects from fields. Some eat clams and mussels. A gull will pick a clam up in its bill, carry it into the air, and then drop it on a rock to break the shell. Gulls are among the few birds that have

When the Eagles Are the Pirates

Some birds steal food from others. Among these "pirates" is the North American bald eagle. Its victim is often the osprey, also known as the fish hawk. The osprey snatches fish from the water with its claws, and then it flies to a perch to eat. An eagle that spies an osprey flying with a fish in its claws will harass it. Since an eagle is larger and more powerful than an osprey, the osprey usually drops the fish. An eagle will often catch the fish in midair and take it to a quiet place to be eaten.

Gulls are among the few species of birds that have benefited from human activities. They often feed at garbage dumps and, out at sea, behind fishing boats, from which fish parts are thrown into the water.

benefited from human activities. Gulls flock to garbage dumps and other areas, such as behind fishing boats, where there is a high concentration of food waste.

A vast number of birds eat insects. Warblers pick insects off leaves. Thrushes often search for insects on the ground. The phoebe perches on a branch and waits for an insect to fly near. Then it darts into the air and snaps up the prey. Swallows like to sweep through the air, catching insects on the wing.

Connections with Other Animals

Some insect-eaters rely on the help of other animals to get food. The oxpecker of Africa often sits on the backs of rhinos and water buffalo, but the rhinos and the buffalo don't mind. Oxpeckers pick tiny parasites off the skins of these large animals. The cattle egret follows behind buffalo and domestic cattle. As the cattle move through the grass, they stir up the insects on which the egret feeds.

Woodpeckers chisel holes into tree trunks in search of wood-boring insects. A woodpecker has a

long tongue, covered with barbs, that points backward. The long tongue hooks insects and drags them out of the holes to be eaten.

Seeds and fruit of all kinds also furnish birds with food. Dark-eyed juncos pick up seeds that fall to the ground. Parrots take seeds, nuts, and fruit off trees. Orioles also like fruit and are fond of nectar. Hummingbirds have long bills and even longer tongues that reach deep into flowers to get nectar.

A Look at the Bill

You can usually tell what a bird eats by the design of its bill. Seed-eaters have short, heavy bills. The hawfinch, a European seed-eater, can crush fruit pits with a force of up to 100 pounds (45 kilograms) per square inch. The red-tailed hawk has a hooked bill, powerful and sharp, for tearing flesh. The spear-like bill of the great blue heron is adapted for catching fish. The woodpecker's bill is short but sharp, like a chisel. The warbler has a short, thin bill. It works like a pair of tweezers, picking insects from plants. Because catching

You can usually tell what a bird eats by looking at its bill. A long, spear-like bill, like the stork's (*below, left*), is best for catching fish. A hooked bill, like the vulture's (*below, center*), is a powerful and sharp tool for tearing up and eating meat. A chisel-shaped bill, like the woodpecker's (*below, right*), is the most effective for chipping away at wood.

Inside and Outside: Bird Anatomy

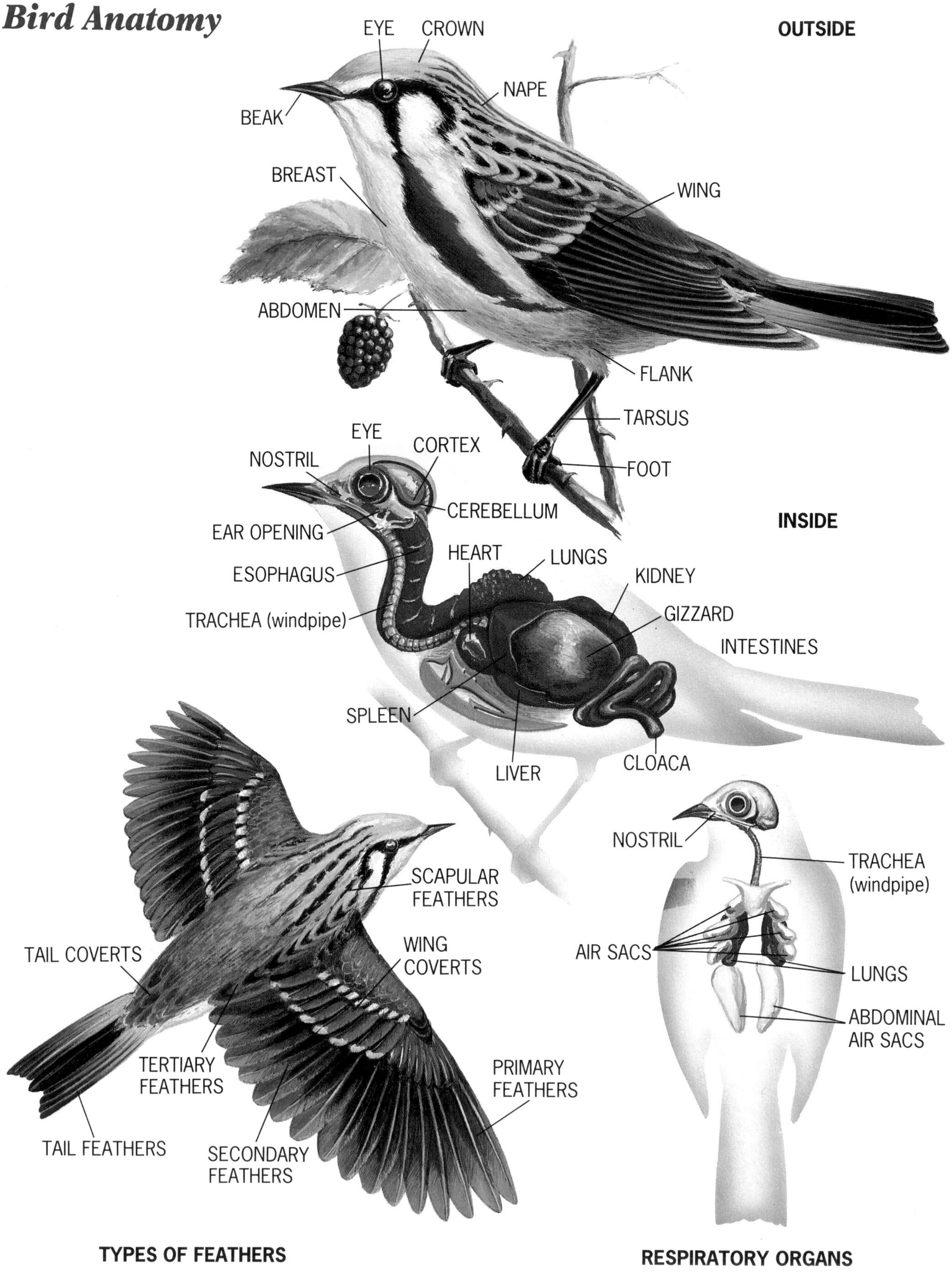

OUTSIDE

EYE
CROWN
NAPE
BEAK
BREAST
WING
ABDOMEN
FLANK
TARSUS
FOOT

INSIDE

EYE
NOSTRIL
CORTEX
CEREBELLUM
EAR OPENING
ESOPHAGUS
HEART
LUNGS
KIDNEY
GIZZARD
TRACHEA (windpipe)
INTESTINES
SPLEEN
LIVER
CLOACA

TYPES OF FEATHERS

SCAPULAR FEATHERS
TAIL COVERTS
WING COVERTS
TERTIARY FEATHERS
PRIMARY FEATHERS
TAIL FEATHERS
SECONDARY FEATHERS

RESPIRATORY ORGANS

NOSTRIL
TRACHEA (windpipe)
AIR SACS
LUNGS
ABDOMINAL AIR SACS

insects in midair requires a scoop-like bill, that's what the swallow has. The lower part of the black skimmer's bill looks like a garden trowel, as the bird flies over the water scooping up fish.

How Birds Digest Food

Most mammals chew food with teeth before it goes through their digestive system. Chewing begins the process of breaking down food. Most reptiles swallow food whole or in chunks. Their digestive system must work harder than a mammal's to break down food.

Birds are in between. They lack teeth, but they can partially chop and cut food with their bills. And most birds have a special structure called a gizzard that substitutes for teeth. The gizzard is most highly developed in plant-eaters. Seabirds do not have gizzards.

The gizzard has hard, muscular walls that have many folds. The walls grind up food as it passes through so that the food is more digestible. Many birds swallow gravel and grit, which go to the gizzard and help to grind the food as well.

Ground-up food goes from the gizzard to the stomach. There, chemicals called enzymes, which

Raising a Good Crop

The faster a bird eats, the quicker it can get back under cover and away from enemies. Fast eating overloads the digestive system, but many birds can get around this problem. A bird's esophagus—the tube leading from the mouth to the stomach—is specially adapted for storing food. Its walls are elastic and thin, and they expand to hold food for later digestion. The lower part of the tube, in many birds, is permanently expanded. This pouch is called a crop. The crop of even a small bird can hold 2 to 3 ounces (57 to 85 grams) of food. Biologists examine the crops of dead birds to find out what they have been eating. Crop contents show what a bird depends on for food at various times of the year. Crop contents also give scientists valuable information about the life cycle and environment of birds.

are produced by glands, break the food down even more. The food breaks down into molecules that can interact with other molecules in the body.

From the stomach, the food molecules go to the small intestine. They then pass through the walls of the small intestine and into the blood.

Material that cannot be digested, such as fur, forms pellets in the bird's digestive system and is spit out from the mouth. Waste from digested food passes through the large intestine and out the anus, which opens at a chamber called the cloaca. Bird urine, which is liquid, from the bird's kidneys, also passes out at the anus.

How a Bird Breathes

Not only are birds eating machines, but they are also breathing machines. They need a great amount of oxygen to make energy. Some birds breathe 200 times a minute while flying. A resting bird breathes about 50 times a minute. In comparison, a human at rest takes only about a dozen breaths a minute.

When a bird inhales, air carrying oxygen enters through nostrils in its bill. The air then passes through the windpipe (trachea) into the lungs.

The process of breathing is almost identical for all animals with lungs. Oxygen from fresh air goes into blood vessels in the lungs. At the same time, carbon dioxide waste passes from the blood into the lungs. When a bird (or a human) exhales, it expels carbon dioxide waste back into the air.

The more fresh air that circulates through the lungs, the more oxygen a bird gets. A bird's lungs are connected to several air sacs. Air rushes through the lungs and into the sacs. Then it goes from the sacs back to the lungs and helps to regulate a bird's body temperature. The sacs extend into the chest, wings,

DID YOU KNOW

Breathing with Muscles

A bird's lungs are not as flexible as a human's. They expand and contract only slightly on their own. However, a bird's powerful chest muscles pump the lungs to draw in and expel air. The movement of the wings also helps to work a bird's lungs.

and other parts of the bird's body. Like balloons, the sacs help to keep a bird in the air.

The Heart of a Bird

The heart of a bird, like that of a mammal, has four chambers. Each heart has two atria and two ventricles. The heart's right side receives used, deoxygenated blood, and the left side sends reoxygenated blood through the body.

Blood vessels called veins bring blood to the heart. Vessels called arteries carry blood from the heart through the body.

When veins take oxygen-depleted blood to the heart, the blood enters the right atrium. It then passes to the right ventricle. Next it flows through a large artery to the lungs for oxygen.

Oxygenated blood goes through other veins to the left atrium and then flows to the left ventricle. A big artery, the aorta, sends the reoxygenated blood to the body.

Because a bird has a high rate of metabolism, its heart has to work hard to keep oxygen and blood moving through its body. A human heart beats about 70 times a minute. A crow's beats about 340 times, and the hearts of some hummingbirds beat more than 1,000 times a minute!

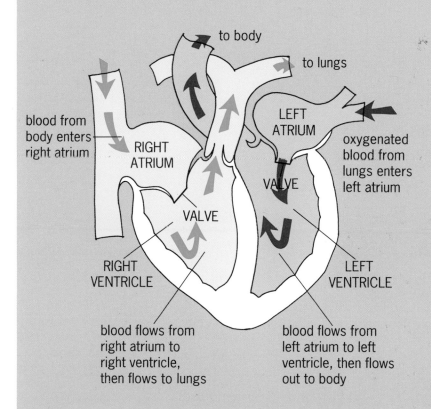

The Four-Chambered Heart

to body

to lungs

blood from body enters right atrium

RIGHT ATRIUM

LEFT ATRIUM

oxygenated blood from lungs enters left atrium

VALVE

VALVE

RIGHT VENTRICLE

LEFT VENTRICLE

blood flows from right atrium to right ventricle, then flows to lungs

blood flows from left atrium to left ventricle, then flows out to body

A bird's heart has four chambers: the right atrium, the right ventricle, the left atrium, and the left ventricle. Blood flows through the right side of the heart on its way to the lungs, where it picks up oxygen and releases carbon dioxide as waste. Oxygenated blood then flows to the left side of the heart, which pumps the blood out to all parts of the body.

4

Reproduction and Growth

Two red-shouldered hawks circle high overhead on an early spring day. Wings outspread, they soar around each other. Then, one folds its wings and falls earthward. It suddenly breaks its dive. With a few powerful strokes of its wings, it rises. Reaching the other hawk, it begins to soar again.

The hawks are male and female. Their aerial acrobatics are a mating dance that prepares them to breed so that they can have young.

Having young is called reproduction. The term *reproduction* means producing new members of a species. All species must be able to reproduce at least as many individuals as are lost to death. If a species cannot reproduce fast enough, it will disappear, or become extinct. That is true for all living things, including humans.

Opposite:
Two yellow warbler parents tend to their newborn chicks. The process by which organisms create new members of a species is one of the most important for all living things.

Changes in a bird's surroundings make its body ready for reproduction. More daylight in spring is one such change. It causes a bird's body to produce certain chemicals that help the bird to make sex cells—sperm in males, and eggs in females. Spring is the breeding season for most birds.

Finding a Mate

In order to reproduce, a bird needs a partner of the opposite sex. Birds use many methods to find and attract partners.

Colors help to bring mates together. Birds can recognize members of their species by feather color and patterns. Colors also identify a bird's sex. Males are often more colorful than females. The female house finch, for instance, is dull brown with dark streaks on her breast. The male, however, has a bright red breast that gets even brighter during the breeding season. When an egret is ready to breed, it sprouts long plumes. The bill of the puffin, a seabird, blossoms into red and yellow. The green head of the male mallard shines like metal. The male bobolink is brownish yellow in the winter. When he breeds, he is black and white.

Sound is another way birds call attention to themselves. Bird songs, usually sung by males, often signal that a bird wants a mate. A song also identifies the singer's species and sex and tells others where it is. And, though it can sound pretty, a bird's song warns any competition to stay away. Because of mating rituals, many bird sounds are most beautiful in the spring. But not all mating sounds are melodious. The male jackass penguin, for example, bobs its head and brays loudly, just like a jackass.

The ruffed grouse lives in woodlands of the northern United States and Canada. The male grouse

An egret sprouts long plumes when it is ready to breed. Many birds use visual displays to find and attract mates.

drums to attract a mate and to warn other males to stay out of his territory. First, the grouse finds a fallen log to be used as his drumming perch. Fluffing out the ruff of feathers around his head and neck, he stands on the log. Then he begins to flap his wings, faster and faster. As they beat against the air, the wings make a loud drumming sound that grows in volume and speed. When the grouse really gets going, his drumming can be heard up to 1 mile (2 kilometers) away. Some people think the grouse's drumming sounds like a chainsaw motor. Others think the drumming of a grouse in the woods is not only beautiful, but also one of the most thrilling sounds of spring.

Mating Displays

The drumming behavior of the grouse is a "mating display." Many birds, such as the red-shouldered hawk, use them. In some species, only males display. In others, both sexes do.

Sandhill cranes flap their huge wings and jump about for their mating display. Sometimes they leap more than 12 feet (4 meters) into the air. The male mallard bobs his head and ducks it in the water. The male redwing blackbird raises bright red-and-yellow wing patches to attract attention.

The males of some species gather together and compete for the attention of females. Every year, they return to the same dancing ground, or lek, to "show off" in an effort to impress the females.

The ruff, a European shorebird, is one species that gathers at a lek every year. The lek is a circle about 6 feet (2 meters) across. After years of use, it is tramped bare of grass. Each year, about a half-dozen males gather at the lek. The male ruff has a huge collar of feathers with two large tufts that rise from his head. His face is vivid red or yellow.

During mating season, the male ruffed grouse fluffs out his feathers and flaps them to make a loud drumming sound. This drumming is meant to attract a mate and to warn other males to stay away.

Males win stations, or courts, in the lek by fighting. They peck, kick, and hit one another with their wings. This behavior seldom causes injuries. When females arrive, the males spread their ruffs, raise their tufts, and bow and bend. When a female picks out a male, she steps into his court. Then the two birds mate.

Migration

Many birds spend the winter in the tropics. In the spring, they go north, where they reproduce. This seasonal travel is called migration. Birds are not the only animals that migrate. Gray whales, for instance, mate off the coast of Alaska and then have their young in the warmer Mexican waters.

The male ruff has a large collar of feathers that provides a dramatic display for females at the lek during mating season.

Some animal migrations cover huge distances. The arctic tern breeds in the far north, then heads south, for Antarctic waters. In total, it is a 22,200-mile (35,726-kilometer) round trip. Most North American songbirds winter far south in the tropics. The bobolink, for example, migrates all the way from the northern United States to Brazil.

The migration to breeding grounds is timed to the arrival of spring. Many shorebirds breed in the Arctic. When they leave wintering areas in South America, the Arctic is still snowbound. By the time the birds get there, however, the Arctic spring has begun, and insect and plant foods are available.

Mating

For many animals, a bond develops between the male and the female as a result of their mating behavior. Once this bond has been created, the two are ready to mate. A bird's reproductive system opens at the cloaca. Birds mate by touching cloacas. There, sperm from the male enters the female and fertilizes an egg. A hard shell forms around the egg before it is laid. Most females lay their eggs a day after they have been fertilized.

Life in an Egg

A growing bird in an egg—like a growing human in a uterus—is called an embryo. A bird embryo is fed and protected inside the egg. The embryo begins as a fertilized sex cell on the yolk. Around the yolk is the white of the egg, called the albumen. The albumen is almost all water. It keeps the yolk and embryo moist and also cushions against shock.

Just under the shell of the egg are two tough membranes. They keep out germs. Oxygen, however, passes through the shell and the membranes.

The shell of a bird's egg is mostly made of calcium carbonate, which is the main component of limestone.

DID YOU KNOW

Love Tokens

Some birds give their mates gifts. The male kingfisher often brings a fish to the female he wants to win over. Other birds offer insects or berries to their mates.

Penguin Pops

After a female emperor penguin lays her egg, she is hungry. To reach her supply of food at sea, she must cross miles of icy tundra (treeless plain). But someone has to incubate (keep warm) her egg while she is gone. That is her mate's job. The male emperor penguin holds the egg between his legs to keep it off the ice. A flap of skin covers the egg. His body heat keeps the egg warm even when the air temperature is far below zero. The male emperor penguin keeps turning the egg over to keep it evenly heated. He cannot leave the egg, because it would freeze in seconds. This means he cannot look for food and must live off his body fat. After six weeks, the female returns, just as the egg is about to hatch. Then the hungry male can go to sea for some food of his own.

A female Canada goose sits and incubates her eggs while her mate stands guard. In most species, both males and females take turns incubating their eggs.

A mammal's embryo develops inside the mother, where her body provides it with food and warmth. A bird embryo, however, feeds on the egg yolk. It is kept warm by a process called incubation.

During incubation, a parent bird sits on the egg. In most species, both parents take turns incubating. The parents protect the egg as their body heat keeps the embryo warm.

You might think feathers would prevent a parent's body heat from reaching the egg, but during incubation many birds lose feathers on a patch of skin on their abdomen. This bare patch is what comes in contact with the egg.

Nestlings (newborn birds) cannot maintain their own body temperature for the first few weeks of life. The parents nest with them to keep them warm. This behavior is called brooding.

The Old Nest Egg

A bird nest is a cradle for eggs and young. Each bird builds its own kind of nest. Some nests are incredibly large and complex. Others are simple and sturdy. There are as many kinds of nests as there are kinds of birds. Each is special in its own way. Barn swallows build mud nests lined with grass and feathers. Bank swallows dig burrows, several feet long, in earthen banks. Some terns lay their eggs on the sand. Their eggs are sand-colored and are hard for predators to see. Many songbirds, like the robin, build cup-shaped nests of twigs and grasses. Weaverbirds in Africa build nests of plant fibers. They weave fibers together, using complicated knots. Some birds, such as woodpeckers, lay their eggs in tree holes. The golden eagle makes a nest of sticks and branches. Each year, the eagle works on the same nest. Some eagle nests can weigh up to 1 ton (907 kilograms). A songbird called the murre lays her eggs on narrow ledges. The egg is pear-shaped, so instead of rolling off the ledge, it rolls in a circle. A hollow in the ground and some grass make a wild turkey nest. The cowbird doesn't build a nest at all. She lays her eggs in the nest of another species when the parents are away. Without knowing it, another species cares for the cowbird egg and young.

Beginning Life as a Bird

A bird that is ready to hatch has two adaptations for getting out of its egg. One is a strong muscle in the back of its neck. The other is a tiny horn on its upper bill, known as the egg tooth. (Many reptiles have egg teeth, too.) Powered by the neck muscle, a young bird breaks through its shell with its egg tooth. Once the bird is out of the shell, the special adaptations are no longer needed. The neck muscle shrinks, and the egg tooth disappears within a few days of hatching.

Most newly hatched birds are helpless. Their eyes are closed, and they have almost no feathers. The parents must keep these young birds warm and bring them food. For some reason, many seed-eating birds start their young feeding on insects. Perhaps this is because seeds are scarce in spring and insects are high in protein.

Some species of birds have more developed young than others. A newly hatched pheasant, for instance, is covered with feathers. From the very start, it can see and walk around freely.

A robin mother brings food for her young nestlings. Many birds hatch without feathers, and most are helpless.

Kinds of Nests

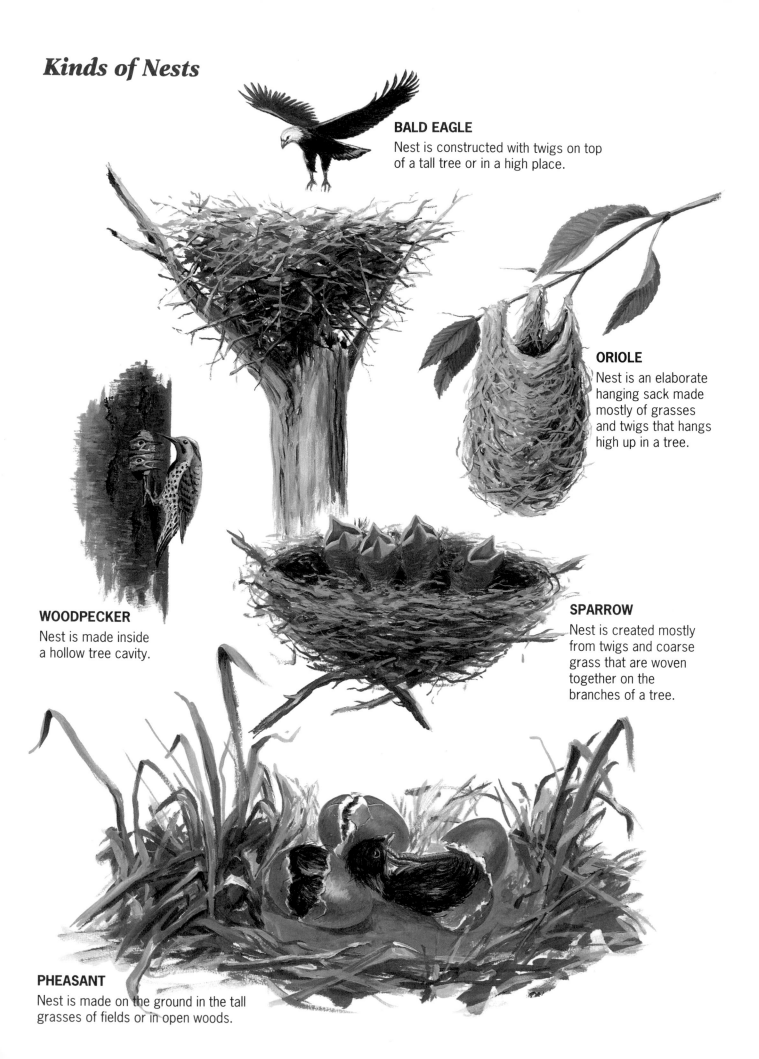

BALD EAGLE
Nest is constructed with twigs on top of a tall tree or in a high place.

ORIOLE
Nest is an elaborate hanging sack made mostly of grasses and twigs that hangs high up in a tree.

WOODPECKER
Nest is made inside a hollow tree cavity.

SPARROW
Nest is created mostly from twigs and coarse grass that are woven together on the branches of a tree.

PHEASANT
Nest is made on the ground in the tall grasses of fields or in open woods.

One thing that characterizes mammals is that they live on milk produced by their mothers. Milk in mammals is produced by the mammary glands (the word *mammal* comes from *mammary gland*). But some birds produce a kind of milk for their young, too. Young mourning doves feed on milk from their mothers. The lining of the mother's crop secretes a liquid called pigeon's milk. (Mourning doves are related to pigeons, which also secrete milk.) The mother dove pumps the milk up from her crop, and the young then insert their bill tips into the base of the mother's bill. A red marking near the spot serves as a usual target for the young. For the first few days of their lives, the baby doves live on the milk, which gives them an especially nutritious head start in life.

Mourning dove with young

Many young birds can feed on their own right away. Young quail pick up seeds and insects, and ducklings feed on small water plants and animals. Young gulls can walk on their own soon after hatching, but they cannot fly. That means they cannot go out to sea to catch food. Instead, their parents hunt for them and return to vomit up semidigested food for their young to eat.

Growing Up Fast

Most young birds grow up fast. A newly hatched European cuckoo weighs a fraction of an ounce. But, nourished by food from its parents, it weighs 50 times more in less than a month.

As a nestling grows, it sprouts feathers. When it is fully feathered, it is ready to fly. Many birds are ready to leave the nest within a couple of weeks, but they may remain several days or even weeks with their parents for protection and food.

5

Fitting into the Web of Life

Not long ago, the American bald eagle, the national bird of the United States, was in danger of extinction in most of the country. As many as 75,000 bald eagles once inhabited the continental United States. By the 1970s, however, there were only a few thousand, perhaps not even that many.

Several factors are to blame for the decrease in eagle populations. In order to survive, bald eagles need wilderness, and since they are largely fish-eaters, they nest near water. They also do not like human disturbance of any kind.

As the United States was settled, eagle habitats were disturbed. Forests were cleared, and eagle nesting trees were lost. In addition, rivers and lakes that were sources of eagle food were polluted or destroyed by the activities of humans.

Opposite:
An American bald eagle flies over a lake in search of fish. For many years, human activities that damaged the eagle's habitat nearly brought the species to extinction in many areas of the United States.

Bald Eagle Eating Habits

Many bald eagles live in and near Yellowstone National Park in Idaho, Montana, and Wyoming. During the summer, 90 percent of their diet is fish. When lakes and rivers freeze, the eagles use another source of food. They catch waterfowl, and they feed on dead elk, deer, and bison.

Environmental Disruption

After World War II, the eagle faced another threat: insect poisons called pesticides, particularly one known as DDT. Pesticides were freely spread on cropland, which then drained into rivers and lakes. There, DDT entered the food chain. The food chain is the natural system by which one organism in an ecosystem feeds on another.

In lakes and rivers, pesticides were absorbed by plants and small creatures. When the fish fed on those plants and creatures, the pesticides got into their systems. Eagles, in turn, ate the fish, and they, too, absorbed the harmful pesticides.

The pesticides poisoned the eagles' reproductive systems. These chemicals caused their eggs to be thin-shelled, making them crush easily. Pesticides also poisoned eagle embryos. As the number of hatchling eagles dropped drastically, it seemed that not enough young would survive to continue the species.

Scientists eventually recognized the great danger of pesticides to the environment. Harmful pesticides were banned, and special wilderness areas were set aside for eagles. Meanwhile, scientists began to raise young eagles in captivity (controlled environments). When grown, many eagles were released into the wild. Now, bald-eagle populations are increasing. They are beginning to show up in places where they have not been seen in years, but it will still be many years before the species completely recovers from the effects of human intervention in its environment.

An Interconnected World

The story of the bald eagle is just one example of how living organisms depend on each other in the natural world. It also shows how all living things depend on a clean and healthy environment.

Many birds depend on other animals for food in order to survive. They eat insects and fish, and several also feed on mammals and other birds.

Every bird has its place in nature. Birds interact with other animals, including humans. Sometimes birds interfere with humans by causing damage to crops or small animals. But birds are also often helpful to humans. If birds did not eat insects, the insect population on Earth would be unmanageable for many humans. Eagles and hawks eat a number of rodents that farmers consider pests.

Natural Enemies

A starving bird is a weak bird, and it is easier for predators to catch. Many animals eat birds and their eggs. Foxes prey on pheasants, and weasels kill nestlings and even large ground birds. Snapping turtles eat ducklings, as do largemouth bass. Some snakes eat birds. The emerald tree boa wraps itself around a branch, blending in with the leaves. When

DID YOU KNOW

Feast or Famine

A bird's food supply varies during the year. Insect-eaters usually nest earlier than seed-eaters. That is because insects are available starting in early spring, and most seeds ripen later. Winter brings a shortage of most bird foods. Some birds, like the Yellowstone eagle, change diets, but migration south solves the food problem for most others.

a bird lands nearby, the boa strikes it. In Africa, there is even a snake that searches the trees and swallows bird eggs whole.

Bird predators also include other birds, such as hawks. The peregrine falcon often catches ducks and pigeons on the wing. Crows and blue jays snatch baby songbirds from their nests and also eat other birds' eggs. Big seabirds called skuas frequently raid penguin nests for food.

Cooperation for Defense in the Natural World

Birds need to stay alert for danger. Have you ever watched a sparrow eating under a bird feeder? It constantly raises its head and looks around. A suspicious shape or movement will send a bird flitting into the nearest bush. The flight of just one sparrow can trigger flight in a whole crowd of other sparrows.

Birds have many behaviors that help to keep them safe from danger. Flying in flocks is a defense tactic for some birds. It is harder for a predator to target an individual bird when it is part of a flock. (Traveling in a school serves the same purpose for fish.)

Many birds find safety in flocks. This is especially true of breeding seabirds. Some seabirds, such as auks, nest in colonies that contain millions of birds. In these enormous groups, there are millions of eyes watching for danger and millions of watchers ready to sound an alarm call if a possible enemy is sighted.

Each species has its own unique alarm calls. Some birds have a special call for a certain predator. A blue jay can even imitate the call of a red-tailed hawk. An alarm call can announce different messages. One message can tell other birds to flee, and another can draw them together.

Many birds, such as shorebirds, find safety in flocks. Some seabirds nest in colonies that contain millions of birds.

Mobbing

Some small birds gang up on their predators. Such behavior is called mobbing. A blackbird may give a mobbing call if a crow comes near its nest. Other blackbirds respond to the call and fly around the crow, making it nervous.

Crows will mob an owl sitting in a tree by daylight. Even a person who walks into a tern colony on a beach may suddenly get dive-bombed by hundreds of nervous, screaming birds.

Fitting into the Web of Life

Air-Traffic Control

BEARDED VULTURE (25,000 feet, or 7,600 meters)

MALLARDS (21,000 feet, or 6,400 meters)

EVENING GROSBEAK (12,500 feet, or 3,800 meters)

EUROPEAN SWIFTS (7,000 feet, or 2,150 meters)

WHISTLING SWAN (4,000 feet, or 1,200 meters)

Although most birds must come down to low altitudes to find food, the many species of birds share the skies by flying at different heights. How high a bird flies depends upon its body structure, feeding patterns, and the habitat below.

ADÉLIE PENGUINS (non-flying birds)

Give Thanks for the Turkey

The wild turkey originally ranged through the forests in most of the United States. Acorns are the turkey's primary food. As forests were cleared, however, the turkey vanished from most of the states. Connecticut lost its last turkey in 1813. Ohio had no wild turkeys by 1880. By the 1930s, only a few groups of turkeys remained, mostly in the South.

Fifty years ago, wildlife biologists began trapping some of the few remaining turkeys. They used a special net to catch whole flocks. At the same time, many forests were regrowing in many areas. Little by little, turkeys were released into these places. The goal was to restore turkey populations so they could once again be legally hunted. Today wild turkeys abound in more than 40 states. Connecticut, for example, now has thousands of them.

Camouflage

Many birds defend themselves with camouflage, which means they blend with their natural surroundings. Feather color, feather patterns, and special behaviors help birds to blend with their environment.

Flipping the Bird

When an owl or a hawk faces a foe on the ground, it spreads its wings and hunches over. It also raises its feathers to make itself look bigger. Birds of prey use their sharp bills and claws to defend themselves as well as to catch food.

Swans and geese defend their nests viciously. The bill or wing of a mute swan can severely injure even an adult human.

The American bittern has two kinds of natural camouflage. Not only does its coloring blend with its surroundings, but its long, thin neck also resembles the reeds in its swampy habitat.

The whippoorwill, grouse, and woodcock are brownish. They nest on the ground and can hide in old leaves. When alarmed, they freeze, which makes them even harder to see.

If danger comes too near, a grouse will explode from under cover. It will rocket into the air as its wings thunder, startling the enemy.

The hen pheasant also nests on the ground. She is brown, too. The cock pheasant has brilliant colors, which attracts females for mating. But he does not sit on the nest. If he did, he would be too easy to spot.

The American bittern is a small heron. It is brown, with a dark stripe on each side of its throat. The bittern lives in moist, swampy places where fields of reeds grow. When frightened, it points its

A Bird for All Seasons

The ptarmigan is a ground bird that lives in cold climates and has a very effective method of natural camouflage. During the summer, its feathers are brown. In winter, the feathers turn white, like snow. This seasonal change helps the ptarmigan blend with its surroundings all year long.

Rock ptarmigan (winter)

Rock ptarmigan (summer)

long bill skyward. In this position, the bird is not easily seen among the reeds. The bittern will even sway to and fro like a reed in the wind.

Birds in Danger

In the past 300 years, at least 44 species of birds have become extinct. The most famous is the dodo. It was a big, flightless pigeon from an island in the Indian Ocean. It was easy to catch, so sailors killed it for food. Pigs that were brought to the island killed more dodos, and rats from the ships ate the young. By the late 1600s, the dodo had died out.

Several species of Hawaiian birds have vanished from a disease that was carried by foreign birds that were released by settlers on the islands.

The Nest Defense...

The killdeer is a small shorebird. The female lays her eggs on the ground, in the open. When an enemy comes near, she fakes injury. Crying loudly, she limps along the ground and drags her wing as if it were broken. This behavior is designed to make an enemy follow her away from her nest. When the enemy is far enough away from the nest, the female killdeer suddenly "recovers" and flies back to her waiting eggs.

Fowl Play

In the jungles of southeast Asia lives a bird called the jungle fowl. It looks just like a chicken. In fact, it is the ancestor of the chicken. The red jungle fowl, pictured below, is the best known of this bird species.

Five thousand years ago, humans domesticated jungle fowl. Chickens were brought to Egypt and Europe by about 1500 B.C. South Seas islanders carried chickens to even the most remote Pacific islands. Today, chickens are found almost everywhere.

About 150 years ago, more than five billion passenger pigeons lived in the forests of eastern North America. Billions were shot for food as the forests were cleared. The last passenger pigeon in existence died in a zoo in 1914.

Today, the greatest threat to birds is pollution and habitat destruction by humans. Many tropical birds—including several kinds of parrots—are threatened by the growth of the pet trade because too many have been taken from the wild. The hunting of game birds is strictly regulated by law in many countries.

Hunting certain ducks whose numbers have declined, for instance, is illegal. But some hunting laws are hard to enforce, and endangered animals still fall victim to poachers, who hunt illegally.

Conservationists and governments around the world are working to save birds in danger. Many birds are protected by law, and several are protected by international treaty. Some, such as the peregrine falcon, have been bred in captivity and released in the wild in order to help their populations stay healthy.

The Human Connection to Birds

Many bird species—and many other animals—have become extinct due to harmful human activities. Pollution and destruction of natural habitats are among the main causes of animal extinction.

Harmful human effects on the natural world can be controlled or stopped. If enough people want them, laws can be passed to enforce the safe disposal of human wastes and to regulate the use of natural resources so habitats are not destroyed. Another way for people to protect endangered animals—especially birds—is to refuse to buy threatened species in pet stores. If no one buys these animals, dealers will not want to capture them.

At home, you can help birds in a number of fun and easy ways. You can plant trees and bushes that will serve as nesting areas or feeding places for local birds. You can even buy a bird feeder—or build one of your own—to provide wintering birds with food while seeds, berries, and insects are scarce. This way, you can help native birds to survive while you observe some of nature's most beautiful and interesting creatures.

During the past 300 years, at least 44 species of birds have become extinct. The dodo (*above*) died out in the late 1600s, when sailors hunted them in great numbers. The resplendent quetzal (*below*) is a small bird that is currently on the list of endangered species.

Classification Chart of Birds

Kingdom: Animal
Phylum: Chordata
Class: Aves

There are approximately 8,600 species of birds that exist today. Scientists commonly classify them into 28 different orders (different authorities use different classifications). The following are 19 orders of the most commonly known birds.

Major Order	Common Members	Distinctive Features
Gaviiformes	loons	divers; legs far to rear of body
Pelecaniformes	pelicans, cormorants	webbed feet, bill for catching fish
Ardeiformes	herons, egrets	long legs, neck, and bill
Anseriformes	ducks, swans, geese	webbed feet, broad bills
Falconiformes	eagles, hawks, falcons, vultures, ospreys	strong talons; sharp, hooked bill
Galliformes	pheasants, turkeys	ground-dwelling, strong legs, spurred feet
Charadiiformes	shorebirds, gulls, terns, auks	varied, some webbed feet, some not; found in or near water
Gruiformes	cranes, bustards	most are long-legged; found in or near water
Apodiformes	hummingbirds, swifts	small, highly specialized fliers, able to hover

Major Order	Common Members	Distinctive Features
Coraciiformes	kingfishers, hornbills	short legs, long bills
Columbiformes	doves, pigeons	short legs; heavy bodies; long, pointed wings
Strigiformes	owls	eyes in front, strong bills and feet, excellent eyesight and hearing; nocturnal
Psittaciformes	parrots, parakeets, cockatoos, macaws	flexible feet, bill used to climb, able to mimic sounds well
Piciformes	woodpeckers, toucans	two toes forward, two backward, chisel-like bill
Passeriformes	perching birds	highly varied, almost 6,000 species; toes automatically lock on perch
Struthioniformes	ostriches	large, flightless, lack a ridge on the breastbone
Apterygiformes	kiwis	medium-sized, flightless, lack a ridge on the breast-bone
Sphenisciformes	penguins	flightless, marine diving birds
Ciconiiformes	herons, stocks, bitterns, flamingos	long legs; wading birds

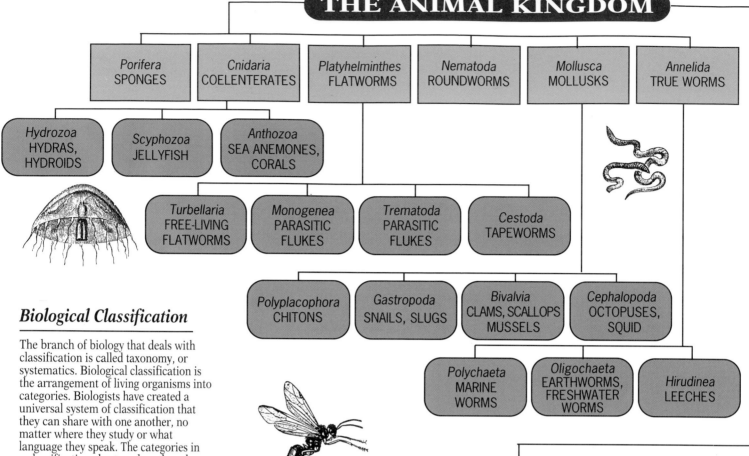

THE ANIMAL KINGDOM

Porifera SPONGES

Cnidaria COELENTERATES

Platyhelminthes FLATWORMS

Nematoda ROUNDWORMS

Mollusca MOLLUSKS

Annelida TRUE WORMS

Hydrozoa HYDRAS, HYDROIDS

Scyphozoa JELLYFISH

Anthozoa SEA ANEMONES, CORALS

Turbellaria FREE-LIVING FLATWORMS

Monogenea PARASITIC FLUKES

Trematoda PARASITIC FLUKES

Cestoda TAPEWORMS

Polyplacophora CHITONS

Gastropoda SNAILS, SLUGS

Bivalvia CLAMS, SCALLOPS MUSSELS

Cephalopoda OCTOPUSES, SQUID

Polychaeta MARINE WORMS

Oligochaeta EARTHWORMS, FRESHWATER WORMS

Hirudinea LEECHES

Biological Classification

The branch of biology that deals with classification is called taxonomy, or systematics. Biological classification is the arrangement of living organisms into categories. Biologists have created a universal system of classification that they can share with one another, no matter where they study or what language they speak. The categories in a classification chart are based on the natural similarities of the organisms. The similarities considered are the structure of the organism, the development (reproduction and growth), biochemical and physiological functions (metabolism and senses), and evolutionary history. Biologists classify living things to show relationships between different groups of organisms, both ancient and modern. Classification charts are also useful in tracing the evolutionary pathways along which present-day organisms have evolved.

Over the years, the classification process has been altered as new information has become accepted. A long time ago, biologists used a two-kingdom system of classification; every living thing was considered a member of either the plant kingdom or the animal kingdom. Today, many biologists use a five-kingdom system that includes plants, animals, monera (microbes), protista (protozoa and certain molds), and fungi (non-green plants). In every kingdom, however, the hierarchy of classification remains the same. In this chart, groupings go from the most general categories (at the top) down to groups that are more and more specific. The most general grouping is PHYLUM. The most specific is ORDER. To use the chart, you may want to find the familiar name of an organism in a CLASS or ORDER box and then trace its classification upward until you reach its PHYLUM.

Insecta INSECTS

Chilopoda CENTIPEDES

Diplopoda MILLIPEDES

Symphyla, Pauropoda SYMPHYLANS, PAUROPODS

Collembola, SPRINGTAILS
Thysanura, SILVERFISH, BRISTLETAILS
Ephemeroptera, MAYFLIES
Odonata, DRAGONFLIES, DAMSELFLIES
Isoptera, TERMITES
Orthoptera, LOCUSTS, CRICKETS, GRASSHOPPERS
Dictyptera, COCKROACHES, MANTIDS
Dermaptera, EARWIGS
Phasmida, STICK INSECTS, LEAF INSECTS
Psocoptera, BOOK LICE, BARK LICE
Diplura, SIMPLE INSECTS
Protura, TELSONTAILS
Plecoptera, STONEFLIES
Grylloblattodea, TINY MOUNTAIN INSECTS
Strepsiptera, TWISTED-WINGED STYLOPIDS
Trichoptera, CADDIS FLIES

Embioptera, WEBSPINNERS
Thysanoptera, THRIPS
Mecoptera, SCORPION FLIES
Zoraptera, RARE TROPICAL INSECTS
Hemiptera, TRUE BUGS
Anoplura, SUCKING LICE
Mallophaga, BITING LICE, BIRD LICE
Homoptera, WHITE FLIES, APHIDS, SCALE INSECTS, CICADAS
Coleoptera, BEETLES, WEEVILS
Neuroptera, ALDERFLIES, LACEWINGS, ANT LIONS, SNAKE FLIES, DOBSONFLIES
Hymenoptera, ANTS, BEES, WASPS
Siphonaptera, FLEAS
Diptera, TRUE FLIES, MOSQUITOES, GNATS
Lepidoptera, BUTTERFLIES, MOTHS

Insectivora, INSECTIVORES (e.g., shrews, moles, hedgehogs)
Chiroptera, BATS
Dermoptera, FLYING LEMURS
Edentata, ANTEATERS, SLOTHS, ARMADILLOS
Pholidota, PANGOLINS
Primates, PROSIMIANS (e.g., lemurs, tarsiers, monkeys, apes, humans)
Rodentia, RODENTS (e.g., squirrels, rats, beavers, mice, porcupines)
Lagomorpha, RABBITS, HARES, PIKAS
Cetacea, WHALES, DOLPHINS, PORPOISES

Carnivora, CARNIVORES (e.g., cats, dogs, weasels, bears, hyenas)
Pinnipedia, SEALS, SEA LIONS, WALRUSES
Tubulidentata, AARDVARKS
Hyracoidea, HYRAXES
Proboscidea, ELEPHANTS
Sirenia, SEA COWS (e.g., manatees, dugongs)
Perissodactyla, ODD-TOED HOOFED MAMMALS (e.g., horses, rhinoceroses, tapirs)
Artiodactyla, EVEN-TOED HOOFED MAMMALS (e.g., hogs, cattle, camels, hippopotamuses)

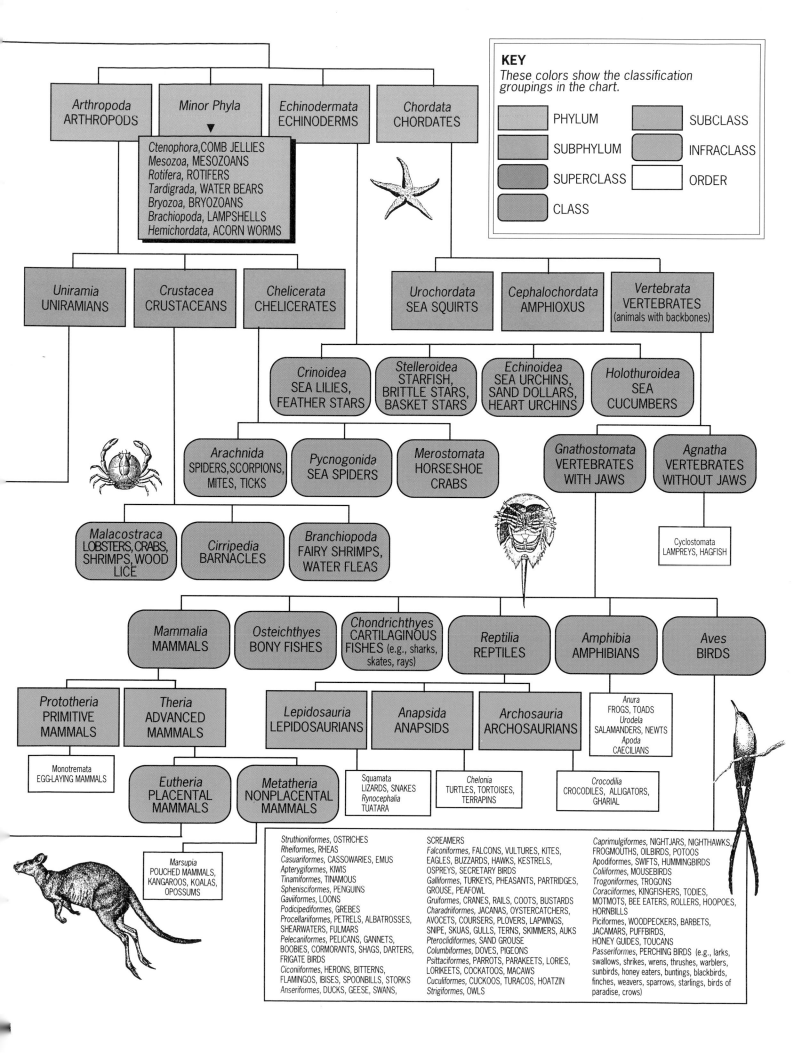

Glossary

adaptation The body part or behavior that helps an organism survive in its environment.

albumen The white of an egg.

aorta A large artery that carries blood from the heart to the rest of the body.

archosaurs A group of ancient reptiles from which birds evolved.

atria The two top chambers of the heart, through which blood flows to the ventricles.

barbs The long, "feathery" parts of a feather.

binocular vision Seeing in three dimensions.

brooding Nesting with young in order to keep them warm.

camouflage The colors, shapes, or structures that enable an organism to blend with its surroundings.

captivity Living in a controlled environment.

cloaca A chamber at which the anus opens.

cochlea A tube-like structure in a bird ear that sends messages to the brain.

cones Light-sensitive cells in the eye that are most sensitive in bright light and register color.

crop A storage chamber for partially digested food.

digestion The mechanical and chemical break-down of food into substances the body can use for growth and energy.

down The soft, simple feathers of a bird.

ecosystem A system formed by the interaction of a community of organisms with their environment.

egg tooth A tiny horn on a newborn bird's upper bill, used for getting out of an egg.

embryo The young animal developing within an egg.

enzyme A substance that breaks down food through-out the digestive system.

esophagus The structure through which food passes from the mouth to the stomach.

extinct No longer in existence.

feces Solid wastes produced by an animal.

food chain The order in which a series of organisms feed on one another in an ecosystem.

gizzard An organ with hard, muscular walls that grinds up food as it passes through the digestive system.

incubate To keep an organism warm while it is developing.

lek A dancing ground used for mating displays.

lens A clear structure at the center of the eye through which light passes to the retina.

mammary gland An organ in female mammals that produces milk.

metabolism The chemical processes in cells that are essential to life.

migration The seasonal movement of animals.

mobbing The behavior whereby a whole group of birds gangs up on a predator.

molecule The smallest particle of a substance that retains all the properties of the substance.

nestling A newborn bird.

nictitating membrane The "third eyelid" of a bird, which keeps the eyes moist and protected.

optic lobe The part of the brain that is involved in vision.

optic nerve One of a pair of nerves that send visual stimuli to the brain.

pecten A structure in the eye of some large birds that supplies extra blood to the eye.

pesticides Chemicals used to kill insects that are considered harmful to humans.

predator An animal that kills other animals for food.

prey Animals that are eaten by other animals.

reproduction The process by which organisms create other members of their species.

respiratory system A system of organs that enables an organism to breathe.

retina A light-sensitive coating on the back of the eye, like the film of a camera.

rods Light-sensitive cells in the back of the eye that are most sensitive in dim light and register only black and white.

species A group of organisms that share more traits with one another than with other organisms and that can reproduce with one another.

stimuli Messages received by an animal's senses from its surrounding.

tundra A treeless plain of arctic and subarctic regions.

urine A liquid waste produced during metabolism.

uterus The female organ in which the embryo develops.

ventricles The two lower chambers of the heart that accept blood from the atria.

vertebrate An animal with a backbone.

yolk The food for a developing embryo in an egg.

For Further Reading

Bailey, Jill. *Save the Macaw*. Milwaukee: Raintree Steck-Vaughn, 1990.

Bailey, Jill, and Seddon, Tony. *Birds of Prey*. New York: Facts On File, 1988.

Brooks, Bruce. *Nature by Design*. New York: Farrar, 1991.

Brooks, Bruce. *Predator*. New York: Farrar, 1991.

Burne, David. *Bird* (Eyewitness Books). New York: Alfred A. Knopf, 1988.

Cherfas, Jeremy. *Animal Builders*. Minneapolis: Lerner Publications, 1991.

Cherfas, Jeremy. *Animal Navigators*. Minneapolis: Lerner Publications, 1991.

Kerrod, Robin. *Birds: Water Birds*. New York: Facts On File, 1989.

Losito, Linda. *Birds: Aerial Hunters*. New York: Facts On File, 1989.

Losito, Linda. *Birds: The Plant- and Seed-Eaters*. New York: Facts On File, 1989.

McConoughey, Jana. *Bald Eagle*. New York: Crestwood House, 1983.

Minelli, Giuseppe. *Dinosaurs and Birds*. New York: Facts On File, 1988.

Olsen, Penny. *Falcons and Hawks*. New York: Facts On File, 1992.

Oram, Liz, and Baker, Robin. *Bird Migration*. Milwaukee: Raintree Steck-Vaughn, 1992.

Patent, Dorothy Hinshaw. *Pelicans*. New York: Clarion Books, 1992.

Patent, Dorothy Hinshaw. *Where Bald Eagles Gather*. New York: Clarion Books, 1990.

Peters, Lisa Westberg. *Condor*. New York: Crestwood House, 1990.

Tesar, Jenny. *Shrinking Forests*. New York: Facts On File, 1991.

Index

Photo Credits

Cover and title page: ©G.C. Kelley/Photo Researchers, Inc.; p. 6: ©Karl Weidmann/Photo Researchers, Inc.; p. 10: ©Bill Curtsinger/Photo Researchers, Inc.; p. 11 (top): ©Leonard Lee Rue/Photo Researchers, Inc.; p. 11 (bottom): ©Stephen Dalton/Photo Researchers, Inc.; p. 12: ©Tom McHugh/Photo Researchers, Inc.; p. 13: ©Phil A. Dotson/Photo Researchers, Inc.; p.16: ©Richard R. Hansen/Photo Researchers, Inc.; p. 19: ©Tom & Pat Leeson/Photo Researchers, Inc.; p.20: ©Jeff Lepore/Photo Researchers, Inc.; p. 21: ©G.R. Austing/Photo Researchers, Inc.; p. 22: ©Lawrence Migdale/Photo Researchers, Inc.; p. 23: ©Tom McHugh/Photo Researchers, Inc.; p. 24: ©J.M. Labat/Photo Researchers, Inc.; p. 27: ©S.R. Maglione/Photo Researchers, Inc.; p. ©Rafael Macia/Photo Researchers, Inc.; p. 29 (top): ©Tom & Pat Leeson/Photo Researchers, Inc.; p. 29 (bottom left): ©Tom McHugh/Photo Researchers, Inc.; p. 29 (bottom middle): ©Jany Sauvanet/Photo Researchers, Inc.; p. 29 (bottom right): ©Gregory K. Scott/Photo Researchers, Inc.; p. 34: ©Alvin E. Staffan/Photo Researchers, Inc.; p. 36: ©M.H. Sharp/Photo Researchers, Inc.; p. 37: ©Nell Bolen/Photo Researchers, Inc.; p. 38: ©Tom McHugh/Photo Researchers, Inc.; p. 40: ©Jeff Lepore/Photo Researchers, Inc.; p. 41: ©Arthur C. Twomey/Photo Researchers, Inc.; p. 43: ©Robert Lee/Photo Researchers, Inc.; p. 44: ©Tom & Pat Leeson/Photo Researchers, Inc.; p. 47: ©Hal H. Harrison/Photo Researchers, Inc.; p. 49: ©Tom & Pat Leeson/Photo Researchers, Inc.; p. 51: ©Leonard Lee Rue/Photo Researchers, Inc.; p. 52: ©Jim Zipp/Photo Researchers, Inc.; p. 53 (left): ©Richard H. Smith/Photo Researchers, Inc.; p. 53 (right): Tom & Pat Leeson/Photo Researchers, Inc.; p. 54: ©Tom McHugh/Photo Researchers, Inc.; p. 55 (top): George Bernard/Photo Science Library/Photo Researchers, Inc.; p. 55 (bottom): ©Tom McHugh/Photo Researchers, Inc.

Technical illustrations: ©Blackbirch Press, Inc.